Inner child rising

Kori Lee

BookLeaf
Publishing

Presentation by *BookLeaf Publishing*

Web: www.bookleafpub.com

E-mail: info@bookleafpub.com

ISBN: 9789395755030

First edition 2022

DEDICATION

My children whom have loved me
unconditionally & who I live for-

& also my beautiful mother who has always
encouraged me to write.

Overfilled

He lights a cigarette - the windows up
 my heart flutters a beat
He's not supposed to fill my cup
Yet it overflows round me

I'm certain of the things I saw
The dress was white the sun was melting
I knew his hand was locked in mine
I knew he must have felt me

When life is like a dream
It seems
Less fear In waking up
When the right one stands beside you
Ain't so damn scary standing up

So done waiting for the catch
Relief in ways it's stayed the same
Getting stronger
trusting actions
The way it should have always been

Hallelujah to the highest
Humble hands will give their thanks
Had to learn so many lessons til I was fit
To love a king

I can promise this day forward
You'll never have to cry alone
Even if not mine for fixin
Two is always easier than one

Facing demons, wielding weapons that
We're forged within a love
The kind that lasts forever and a day
No thought or chance of giving up

Envy will of course rain round us
Jealous people setting traps
Fork in hand waiting to eat us
We'll make them starve to death like that

Marry me today and every day
Sit back and watch us chase our dreams
 as a team working together
We'll make them all realities

When we're old and skin is leathered
And our time on earth faces it's end
We'll sit in rocking chairs together
Still in love the best of friends

The little band around my finger
All the love grown from the start
Cherish memories we made together

Hand in hand and heart in heart

Marry me today and every day
For you will rule my heart forever
Never felt a love like this
Im certain fate brought us together

King of kings

Please tell me that this love is real
For I have surely grown so tired
Surviving trying hard to heal
It is my one desire
To learn to put my weapons down
Not have to watch over my shoulder
Shield and sword tucked safe away
For in love I would grow bolder
I'd only have to pick up arms
When needing to protect
True loves kiss or in defense of it
Sure claws straight for the neck
Of any enemy who showed envy
Desiring to take one of our thrones
No amount of perseverance
Could rattle the weakest of loves bones
Sewing plans and making dreams
I'll love the things in you , you can't
 I'll be the queen & you the king of kings
There will not be a thing we can't
Figure out if we're together
Two heads are better than just one
Between our hearts will be a tether
 not even death could
Wish undone

Will excitement of the new wear off
Once every square inch of my skin is touched
Will you hunger for another on days You feel
my flaws are just too much
Ponder deep before you speak
Your answer must not carry the what ifs
For what it means to me is everything
Cling tight When thin comes after thick
I've yet to meet my match in ability
loving fierce and loving true
Loyalty in me unfaltering
No others noticed in the room
So will you cherish me
 kiss with lips that only speak In truthfulness
Think you might could share a reign
And battle for a love unlike the rest
My heart I put inside your hands the rest I leave
to you
I want a love like this forever
In darkness hands down Id
still choose you

Guardian

Spirit tells me you're a guardian
Soul older than you'd know
Sent here to live a human life
Keep watch on loved ones souls

Hardships you have made it through
Early years - a roller coaster in your mind
Raising 5 wild children & one made an angel in
the sky

You spoke of memories so patiently
Never gave yourself the credit
I know your life was hard on you
Though you'd never have said it

Your Witt runs through my very veins
Eyes see more than what they've said
Tried your best to tend to others
They should have cared for you instead

Like me & my procrastination - they'll always
be the time one day
No returning of the calls that I kept on saying
I wound make

Regret is oh so heavy
Now it's To late to make it right
What I wouldn't give for one more look
Upon your aura light

I know that you're in peace now
Would never want to see me cry
But grief is what I feel in me
Disassociations how I'll hide

What ifs go on forever
wish I'd have been there in the end
Talk you out of that stubbornness
That my veins too are carryin'

I'm sorry that when your soul left -
Your vessel lay there all alone
With no one there to help you
Or pray for you as you went home

I've got your jewelry box - my favorite
I'll never ever let it go
I love you and how I'll miss you
I wish I would have told you so

Be

I've seen the future, good and bad
What bitter sweet visions I've had
Come the end I wasn't sad
The vivid things I've seen

It isn't easy to admit
but next to me is where you stood
I'll let you lead if you just could
Help me water things we plant

For once my love begins to grow
It multiplies out of control
Calmed only by another soul
That sees me in the dark

For when upon me darkness creeps
There's no amount of counting sheep
That can ever quite put me asleep
No one sees -
how storms -
they pass

If someone would believe in me
I'm certain of what I could be
Someone that lets my wild free

Yet connected to my roots
They'd see
I'll do the things I should

 The things I crave aren't out of reach
Passion, trust , to learn , to teach
Kind in ways we disagree
Remembering to BE.
Always
Remembering to BE.

So if you think you might just love me
Make sure those words be true
'Cus I might do something crazy like
Let my walls fall for you

Wake up in your bed

I've wondered what it felt like to wake up in
your bed
 Some how I know it would feel right
Once I layed down my head

Synchronies in breathing I'm sure I'd count each
breath we took
Watch your eyelids dreaming
I bet your hearts an open book

If you woke up frightened with sweat and tears
from dreams unseen
Your terrors from the nighttime would be lulled
away by me

I've often wondered what it felt like to be the
one your eyes searched for
The first thing to rest your gaze on
Each time you came through the door

But I don't think that you've seen me
Or maybe it's just not meant to be
But I'll keep wishful thinking
That one day you might fall for me

I have wondered what it felt like
 on the other side of walls and locks
I know I'd love you like the ocean
Find beauty inside things you are not

A stubborn heart won't heed convincing
Shut doors that hold no keys
Unopened to the thought of love
Or are you just closed off to me

I have wondered what it feels like
For me To wake up in your bed
I just know that it would feel right
You'd be the home I could rest my head

Whatever's meant to be will be

You see whatever's meant to be will be
Fate that's guided by our choices
Always make their way to happen
No matter the loud objecting voices

Pretend to see what I can't see that confidence
is so intriguing
When it comes to efforts put in staying
Yet still feels like you are leaving

Alone within your company
Cannot pretend that I enjoy
Not knowing the intentions
As if my body were a toy

Surely not- my soul is sacred seen by
Such a rare few friends
Never open up , can't fake it
How I share it all depends

On your talents of reflecting
Mirror things I love in me
Pretend you also feel it
Then contradict your surety

Showed you the way so won't put blame In you
Though the vibe was not maintained
Slightly annoying but familiar
Every one turns out the same

Think I've finally learned my lesson though
It is so vital to observe
Every word and it's tempo
Any clear purpose that they serve

Or are you talking just to hear it just like you
listen to reply
Communication has its barriers
Tho I cannot comprehend just why

All it takes are ears that listen and a heart- that's
kind and just
Mouth that offers validations
On Ways in which you ache from love

You see whatever's meant to be will be
Please don't misread my heart as cold
Attracted to the thought of being free
Though I gave you this heart to hold

Bed of clouds

Write for me a song with lyrics that
A lover might decode
Then pair it with a melody
Notes equally as bold

While I rest in your bed of clouds
Sing it til I drift to sleep
So I might know what it might feel like
To behold a thing so sweet

Won't know if your eyes watch me
For I'll be much too deep in slumber
Smother me with softness
tuck my body in the covers

You Take my heart with the melody
I take middle of your bed
your very favorite pillow case
Now smells like me instead

Pricks from feathers poking
Can't help but pull the rest right through
Since I'm cold natured I notice
The little things you let me do

But it's not about the special pillow
Or the blanket kept -you see
It's Silent words your eyes have spoken
Each time that you make love to me

Write for me a song with lyrics that
Reach out beyond this planet
Play it over and again
Til I can no longer stand it

Let me

Let me love the man I see
Perfectly imperfect
I see the things destined to be
Certain his heart is worth it

Freedom I will give to you
Can always spread those wings
Fly- so long as you stay true
 & come flying home to me

Let me know the heart I see
The aches the scars the hurt
The things you hide from other loves
Walls built from empty words

Let me kiss those lips that've spent
Too long translating words
Held inside not paying rent
Listening ears unlikely heard

Loyalty I'll give to you
Find our way into the middle
Common grounds met willingly
When two both try a little

Let me hold that inner child
rock him til his shame subsides
Introduce him to my own
Let them walk side by side

Let me put to rest the nightmares that
Reach further than your sleep
Make clear to them I stand with you
With two - they will retreat

Let me love the man I see
Familiar to my wild spirit
Rule our love so tenderly
With no more need to fear it

Muse

Wild feet need rest from running
In the prisons of a mind
Trapped on an earth so stunning
Gifts not of earthly kinds

I seek a muse that's Wit-might- just outmatch
 Though not set to humble me
That I find some growth in just the same
For i have humility

Sometimes ponder ways in which I'm broken
Wonder where normalcy first severed
And the darkness of survival mode
Began making its tethers

I'll set this world on fire you know
Embody desires fit for kings
No matter how deep your darkness goes
I wish to see you free

Wild hearts need loyalty
 and room to grow within
And also in each other
Learning how to love again

queen of wild nature things knows how to
follow lead
If bound to a worthy lover that
She wants but never needs

You surely are my muse it takes one look
When our eyes meet
For me to come unglued
Like there's no force we couldn't beat

My body like the canvas
Finger tips replace the brush
Mouth that speaks to me in truths
Heart & passion that builds trust

Take my hand and give me certainties
put all of my faith in you
Kiss me as if the worlds on fire
I swear I'll love you true

Glory or destruction

The numb has started taking me
Never know just what to do
I feel like love is shaking me
Reminding what is true

Bound in glory or destruction
Which will this life put us through?
I feel as though I'm wrapped in chain
One that's also bound to you

Can you feel my heart that's beating
Can you taste the lips you kiss
Make sense of the pulsations
Surging through lost fingertips

I've seen a life in worlds not this one
Within it trading swords and shields
Joined together found no weakness
Each of us began to peel

The layers back -to solve the riddles
Seeing with sight interpretations
Could be wrong - though if I'm right
We'd -never dabble in temptations

Keep me safe my soul is shaking
Gotten used to life alone
So many promises I'm breaking
Letting myself build a home

When I promised that I'd never Make the same
-mistakes I'd made before
Yet when I'm with you I never tremble
Don't stand with one foot out the door

Please don't ever make me wonder make me
lose my faith or trust
And on nights tempted with loneliness
I hope you sleep - then you wake up

And feel the power from connection
Even when the distance grows
Don't think even for a second
It mustn't heart if I don't know

Damn the depths of intuition
For if you crack I'll get inside
Pick apart chosen omissions
So obvious I analyze

But the key lies in the secrets
and if you twist the truth enough
It will nag and fester in me
Until the truth you've covered up

Sits out displayed - no explanation
Could ever place the balance back
So do not waste a precious moment
Tell me where you're head was at

I surely do not crave perfection
But how I've hungered for a soul
 One full of trust & fierce in loyalty
Peculiarity to break the mold

The world breaks but I still want you
Crave the love engulfed with lust
If you let it die this love will haunt you
Til the day were ash and dust

The numb has started taking me
Trying not to self protect
can't help but be a little scared
Hope my heart - you wont neglect

Different breed

I hope you can manage to see that I'm a different
kind of breed
Wrapped In shades of darker hues
Baptized in -blood of enemies

Though my soul is darker in completion
Time will show where morals reach
Passions to learn from endless mentors
Humble willingness to teach

I've held a crippling starvation where
The hungers never quenched
Relief short lived occasionally
Gone quickly as the winds

The taste of truths bring such mercies
Proving words -flow in abundance yet lack
actions
Binging to purge the shit force fed to me
Monotonous shallow interactions

My metamorphosis emerging
Darkest contents oozing out
Slithering through -find ways to intercept ,
inflicting shreds of doubt

The goodness in the core of me
My willing mind has chose to be
No force dare think it possible to make a slave
of me

Decades practicing stretching each threshold that
the weak couldn't dare to dream they'd have
Creating creeds of moral codes with common
sense
most humans - ignorantly lack

A diamond in the rough forged from the last of
dying breeds
Gifted bitter sweetly in form of paranormal
things

Open up the very eyes you used to overlook -
Ignore
The power united we'd possess
Unmatched by anyone before

The most grim of ends is coming
evil wakes- stirred by eclipse
Deep in slumber
Each and every soul we must awaken
For evils mission is
 to snatch and take us under

Breaking the world

Listen to the world breaking
 we must be careful mustn't move
Come dawn
 the sunlight burns to ash- The binding that
 Late nights hopes have tied onto

With Head start my wild feet -then venture off
No time for sad goodbyes
Almost seduced by ball and chains
Imagining what love might be like

Why do we tempt our fate? the world breaks its
self in two
The mornings promise you'll then make
Just one last night I'll share with you

Cracks into the core of earth split right longside
these hearts
That push and pull each other under blankets
Made of stars

When my Skin touchs your skin
there is no other -I'd even think to let
 or much less crawl
Inside of my scars - short lived elixirs tend -

To the wastelands of my heart

So what if the whole wide world breaks so what
if deserts spread
So what if damned their souls might be
If I wake in your bed

The earth might crumble 'round us certainly
Might face the wrath of burning suns
Atleast we'd share our company
wouldn't have to feel alone

Your wish is my command my love
Come lonely nights I'll find your bed of sins
Then once hope turns into ash
 I'll leave
For its Your world that I live in

Crickets

When I can hear the crickets sing
Wish that I could read minds
Uncertainties the quiet brings
Truth seeks to find the light

Does the pause mean hesitations
Or is it thoughtfulness
Any brand new revelations
That point to paths that hold regrets

Can you feel in me frustrations
No way to skip forward or rewind
And change the vital factors
Or find escape of any kind

From a fate that's lacking fairness
Come back to haunt the now with pasts
No companion to balance carelessness
Creating firsts not learning lasts

I can't let go for there's a magnet
Seems it pulls me close and sure
Unlike the things I'd known before
That have tricked me in seeing good

Calm and steady grows the oak seed
Wait patiently to watch the roots spread strong
Then when sunlight makes limbs ready
Branches become foundations leaves grow on

Born from the loyalty of giving trees growing
like it's limbs
I unlocked & opened up your story
Skimmed through all of your notes in pen

I saw the lips you'd kissed before me
Saw the fears - how each was birthed
Felt the tingles chill bumps raised my skin
From some of the painful things I'd heard

Must've surely noted- feet stayed planted
Didn't flinch through unappealing soiled pages
Never thought to once take cover
When reading folded ears -marked dates of
stormy rages

If you let me I will love you strong, prove the
ways my heart is true
Accept the ways a mind has changed
This soul I'll give to you.

I'd hold your hand past sleeping monsters
Reject those whom wish to share loves bed
I'll Hold your chin up when you can't

On shameful days you hang your head

Wait patiently held off by dreams where our
skins allowed to meet
Write words to you in poetry
Live in truths that set us free

Dreams

Not quite as simple as The end -
 in re-occurring dreams
Putting trust into another imperfect
 and hurting human being

Scales -don't always balance even
Though one should take into account
Scars- exist- though some can't see them
Add too much weight the arms give out

When do you feel the lonely?
What is the threshold til your break?
The point where water cracks foundations
Destroys the dam that hugs the lake

How does one evade ones will?
Conquer a mind as if it's sleeping
Easy as the river flows
Though heavy as a soul that's weeping

Spinning chaos with no control
Tops made not -for standing still
Peace might have the chance at catch-up
If value placed in what was real

Tangible no longer- let it slip through shaky
fingers
Memories hit stronger til my scent no longer
lingers

On the pillows where love rested dreams that
didn't quite take flight
Where truth and trust were bested
Raw mistakes and lonely nights

I'll fade with all the others
though one day I know you'll see
My love unlike another's
Roots of love like cypress trees

I seek the deep you bask in shallows
Lately - tell me why that's changed
Can't speak in truths consistently
Pointless stories re-arrange

I ask too much I argue not
our talking circles spin and spin
Why not agree to disagree
That way we both can take the win

Isn't that what it's about when we play the game
this way
Isn't hard to figure out
The things that make a lover stay

Consistency, conviction, overcoming lonely
nights
the space next to the side of you
Not filled with foolishness or spite

Temporary turns to permanent in terms of
damage done
Real life holds no rewinds
That's why the little lonely sun

Inside of you that feels an appetite
Not a single soul could fill
Until the man inside the mirror
Allows himself to finally heal

You can keep wondering in the darkness
Won't find me on the other side
I'll warn a king ends up a joker
Without a queen to sit beside

But who am I to have opinions
When my value comes and goes on whims
That's why my scent will fade from bedsheets
You'll no longer find me in

Memories slip away and taste less bitter
Hearts heal in their own ways
find joy within your freedoms

& love my memory til it fades

Pandora's box

I told you not to venture
Told you not to look inside
Don't even stop to think of it
Don't dream of it at night

But even with my warnings
The selfishness inside your core
Could not even help itself
Seems it's always taking more

So while I wasn't looking
Drifting far into my dreams
You reached inside my chest and stole
Right out from under me

The master key - that held my darkness
The memories I have long forgot
How did you imagine it would play out
 To open my Pandora's box

Even though your dead eyes showed
The shift to deep regret
I told you I mean words I say -
nothing more
& nothing less

Don't dream of me at nightfall
Think of me each morning light
Don't bother to feel sorry
Don't ever dare apologize

Because you knew what you were doing
Don't pretend you had forgot
I asked for one thing only
To Leave alone Pandora's box

Strength in me

All I know about this strength in me
Is that it comes from all the breaking
When I've felt trapped or others set my love free
strength steadily in making

A savage birthed relentlessly to fight Long side
my sins
To keep alive the core of me
And lend a helping hand

the darkness never wins and when the time
 to see the damage done has come
Too close for comfort few have gotten -though
 Each coward chose to run

Empath in me is frightening - sometimes it's
threatening too
a close minded - one way man
That does not understand the things I feel are
true

a man that has no plan
Uncomfortable within his own skin
Wagering his bluffing hand

A royal flush he's up against

Once I'm gotten where they've wanted
No more chase when there's no rush
Calling every name then they resort
To folding all my secrets up

Chip away a heart of gold
Becomes a focal point for fun
Though an easy target i may seem
I'm learning not to load the gun

All I know about the strength in me
My companion through and through
For when the others run because I see
One day
They will wish
they had it too

Paradox

I play the devils advocate
Pretend that I am strong when Im undone
Walking , living , breathing, contradicting, a
True oxymoron

My storm is unintentional though winds
Have blown some down
Strong winds and clapping thunder
You may love or hate the sound

all the same- barefoot - I stand here
Dripping wet -actions -my own
Sand under my feet, feeling the earth between
my toes

Not -a single one stood up for me
Come time to evade a destructive mind
Yet I've stood there for so many
stood there patient -stood there kind

I must take the blame though - a soft heart
needed cracks to grow some roots
every heartache broke me down
Until from each and every crack I bloomed

I find unity with oceans I've learned to feel the
pulse of trees
Love so fiercely hard and potent
That the moon now speaks to me

Seen a magic in the twilight
Molded a gift out of a curse
Knew the heart that beats in me is certain
The words I speak won't be rehearsed

Never ending learning no not the smartest in the
room
Mother in me yearning to teach my children how
to bloom

Limit those with access kryptonite in form called
friends
Mere acquaintances if truth be told
Loyalty they'll never give

A village I'm collecting- those Souls where it
comes natural To protect
Who's morality never in question
My ideas they don't reject

Who know the hearts of all my children
Little toes dug in the ground
Show them that it's our chosen family
That will not ever let them down

I'll always be the devils advocate
The worst Of my days not soon forgot
But I'll always grow right out of it
A true,walking, breathing -paradox

Fire and Ice

There's wonders in the mountains
Cautions bouncing peak to peak
Of weather that is rolling in
Even the wisest men will heed

Seductive in its nature ice will lace
The world below
Those left without a shelter
Meet their fate beneath the snow

Temperature is steady dropping
Only the moon left in the sky
Mesmerized by lights and cracklings
 spotted on the far tree line

The smoke is thick and quickly spreading
 flames swallowing the Forrest whole
Hot enough to melt the frozen ice
Evaporate the falling snow

 ice never knew such things existed
All her life she had preserved
Each and every memory
Inside a blizzards icey blur

Fire danced & moved around her
He knew patience was the key
For melting her heart slowly
Will keep the ice from sizzling

ice turns into water
Could not without His patient heat
Together boil hotter
Neither left alone to freeze

Caitie

My darling I could not forget
My Memories like an elephants
Lonely days I've surely spent
Now I am glad I don't have to
Our days apart are done and through
You have always loved me true
Like the best of friends should do
You have always loved me true

It's crazy how we blinked one day
Memories flash being replayed
Just like that you moved away
So many years have come and gone

But I have loved you since third grade
So many times my soul you've saved
Friends? You are my longest one
Oh how we used to have such fun

Ride my bike down to your place
Figs ripe- I still recall the taste
You handled me with so much grace
I know how I used to talk too much

Time capsules we put in the ground

Lions, bunnies, and all the sounds
When I played with you I could not frown
Our legs did so much running

Dishing cream from ice boxes
Picking out the whipping switch
Things that I'll never forget
I thank god for your heart

I knew back when you cried to me
How alone was how you'd always be
I told you I envied your free
I was certain you were wrong

Now look at all those little feet
That call you momma looking sweet
So blessed I've had the chance to meet
Those Little pieces or your soul

I don't know how you do it
But yet if someone could -it would be you
You are a superwoman -
To do all the things you do
Don't carry doubt -for I see you

Life it's quite a crazy ride -
know that I'll be there by your side
Be a shoulder -wipe your eyes
Whenever - should you need to cry

Never judge, betray, or lie, I promise -
till the very end
Over 20 years I've called you friend
I promise till the very end

Happy birthday darling dearest
I guess now you've joined the 30s club
I hope it's the best one yet for you
Your heart I'll always love

The moon and sun

Haunting me as if a ghost
I burst with memories
Your ears are steady burning
Though-I bet you don't think of me

What happened to the things we were
Do you think I'd just forget?
We're So much better than that ending
Confusions all you left me with

The story that you've sewn inside
Every square inch of your head
Do you not hurt like me at night?
Replay the words you left unsaid?

I trusted you with all of me
thought we'd surely pass the test of time
Never noticed or did not want to see
Your heart burned cooler than mine

When was it really over what moment did you
know
That you were not infact in love
Wanted to let me go?

Where you all that certain or just sticking to the
plan
When you pulled back the curtain
I surely did not know that man

I'll never know the answers I guess I shouldn't
care to understand
I miss all the little moments
Nights where we were making plans

Why is my heart bleeding so? Wish so badly you
had stayed
Held me instead of letting go
How did our love just wash away

Alive but I still grieve you
This heart has never felt so broken & alone
I'll love you til I push the daisy's up
I wish you'd come back home

I know that might sound crazy
After all that has been done
I am but a lonely moon
My person was the sun